T0042266

My Fish Tank

Belle Perez

The water in my fish tank is dirty.
I need to clean my fish tank.

I use a net to take out my fish.
I put them in a bowl of clean water.

I take out the rocks and plants.

How will I take out the dirty water?

I can use a siphon.
I fill a rubber tube with water.
I pinch the ends of the tube.

I put one end of the tube in the fish tank.
Then I let go of that end.
I make sure the tube stays under the water.

I put the other end of the tube into an empty bucket.

Then I stop pinching the end of the tube.
The water flows out of the tank
and into the bucket.

My fish tank is now empty.

I clean the rocks and plants.
How will I put clean water in the tank?

I can use a siphon to fill the tank.
I fill the tube with water.
I put clean water in a bucket.
Then I put one end of the tube in the bucket.

I put the other end of the tube into the tank.
The water flows out of the bucket
and into the tank.
My fish tank fills with clean water.

I put the rocks and plants in the tank.

I put a new castle in the tank, too!
What else do I need in my fish tank?

My fish!